I0019617

TOR and The Dark Net

Learn To Avoid NSA Spying And Become Anonymous Online

By

Jared Norton

Table of Contents

Introduction 1

Chapter 1: What is the Deep Web and Why Is It Worth

Exploring? 4

Chapter 2: The Only Ways to Surf Anonymously 14

Chapter 3: Pros and Cons of Using Tor................................ 17

Chapter 4: Pros and Cons of VPN 21

Chapter 5: Pros and Cons of Proxies................................. 25

Chapter 6: The Most Common Mistakes Made in Anonymous

Surfing 29

Chapter 7: How to Avoid NSA Spying.................................33

Chapter 8: Anonymous Email.. 43

Chapter 9: Getting Rid of Evidence and History (and Why You

Might Want To).. 46

Chapter 10: What You Might Find on the Dark Market 51

Chapter 11: What Else Can Go Terribly Wrong? 64

Conclusion.. 69

Introduction

"I wasn't careful on the deep web...and I sure paid for it. After surfing around the deep web mindlessly, I was lured into a red room where I saw terrible things being done to innocent human beings! What's worse...a systems administrator began chatting to me. He knew where I lived. Then I saw myself on webcam! Soon, there was a knock on my door...!"

Does this sound familiar?

If you've ever heard outrageous stories about online illegal drug stores, hit men for hire, celebrities busted for child porn, mad scientific experiments, and Illuminati rituals, you've probably heard of the "dark web", alternatively called the deep web.

It's said to be the unchartered web browsing experience, the mysterious and sometimes terrifying "dark side" of the Internet, where you can supposedly find things that are shocking, illegal or highly top secret.

It's a great story for sensationalist news magazines to tackle, especially when you have unconfirmed reports of aliens, cults, murders and other shocking things that no decent human being should ever see. It's also a favorite on YouTube horror and CreepyPasta, since they love adding onto urban legends.

But have you ever wondered if these stories are true? What is the Deep Web or Dark Web, exactly?

It would be foolish to say that all of the things you've heard about the Deep Web are fake.   Some cases have been very unfortunately very real and sometimes publicized.   There really was an online drug market website called Silk Road that was taken down by the FBI.   There have been many instances of pedophiles and murderers being busted by investigating deep web IP addresses and "digital fingerprints".

There have also been well publicized stories of national security secrets and whistle blowing being revealed at the hands of Edward Snowden, Bradley Manning, Julian Assange, the "Anonymous" group of protesters, and many others.

What we do know for sure is that there is plenty happening on the deep web and some of it can be scary.   We also know that curiosity is eventually going to get the better of you and you're going to want to investigate this forbidden zone on your own.

We're here to tell you that, surprise!, it is completely safe and legal to surf the Deep / Dark Web and it's highly unlikely that you're going to be stalked, invited into a Red Room, or arrested by accident for stumbling on the wrong site.

You will find that if you take basic precautions—and more importantly understand how the darknet and deep web operate—you will be less likely to make a mistake.

What we aim to do in this book is show you how to surf anonymously, how to cover your tracks in case you're paranoid, and generally, how to avoid being arrested by doing something insane—which we trust you're not going to do!

By the end, you're going to understand what software you need, what additional precautions you ought to take, and what sites might pose the biggest personal risk and thus should be avoided.

So sit back and click away as we start our journey into the most intimidating place on earth—the unfiltered, hidden Internet!

Chapter 1

What is the Deep Web and Why Is It Worth Exploring?

Words like "deep web" or "dark net" are sometimes used interchangeably although they are altogether different entities. The simple explanation, and the reason why deep and dark are sometimes confused, is that the majority of users only use the "surface web"—the most popular and heavily linked websites on the Internet. That leaves potentially millions of privately owned and operated websites that no one has officially classified or "indexed" (such as what Google and Bing do by crawling public websites), and perhaps only a handful of people have actually seen.

Some individuals have likened the deep and dark web to trying to fish in the ocean, or perhaps an iceberg that rises to the surface but actually goes thousands of leagues under the ocean. As far back as 2001, the deep web was said to be "orders of magnitude" larger than the surface web, and modern 2016 reports suggest that hidden websites and databases are 500+ times greater in number than everything we see on the surface web.

Now theoretically, there are millions of websites that you would ordinarily never find, unless of course, you were able to penetrate the deep and dark web.

What we see with our favorite sites (Facebook, YouTube, etc.) could be called the **filtered media**. You will have access to only filtered information and news information, as well as entertainment pages, which have been carefully selected for your viewing. This is a similar practice to how executives plan network or cable television.

Search sites like Google and Bing may be able to link you to obscure pages that have very low popularity, thanks to a longtail keyword search such as "Historical Records from the 1800s." It may not be a well known page but you can still find it with some diligence.

Sites like LiveLeak and 4Chan are known for sometimes posting controversial content that is later investigated and taken down, but even these sites are still considered the surface web, because they have high traffic (and many people who can report illegal or questionable content) and because many of their pages are searchable.

The deep web refers to sites and pages that have been intentionally blocked from any search engines indexing the content. Also called the invisible or hidden web, these pages and sites are usually not illegal or even dangerous; they're simply not made to be searched. This could include anything from non-public entertainment, or perhaps private content that is password protected, such as online banking records, web mail, pay on demand video or subscription magazines, and various medical or legal documents that are considered non-public information.

It should be noted that there are two ways to avoid being indexed by a search engine; either manually install code (or download an automatic plug-in) that blocks search robots from crawling the webpage, or do not externally link the page (or site) to any other external pages.

Search engine bots find new sites by following a linking trail, page to page, onsite and offsite. Even a website that doesn't advertise and that avoids registering with any public search engine or domain name can still be found via search if it is linked to other public pages.

Deep web pages cannot be searched and thus offer greater privacy than public surface websites. However, these websites still answer to an authority since they are hosted by well known internet service providers that offer private or shared server hosting. While they do have privacy, anything you see on these pages is far from anonymous. There is a long paper trail. Deep web pages can limit access by these technologies:

- Registration and login required

- Unlinked pages

- Non-HTML content, such as multimedia with highly specific file formats

- Scripted content that is only accessible through JavaScript, Flash or other special scripting

- Dynamic content or contextual webpages, which are only returned through a specific form, query or access context

- Search-prohibited code, such as Robots Exclusion programming, or even using CAPTCHAs to disqualify searching bots

In simpler words, the deep web is still theoretically possible to surf, if inconvenient.

The Difference Between the Deep Web and Darknet

What differentiates the deep web from the "dark web" is that the dark web is hidden from the public Internet and is not accessible at all without special software. You cannot accidentally stumble onto the Dark Web. You must take deliberate steps to download the software.

Darknet refers to an overlay network with restricted access, one requiring the use of different communications protocols and ports in configuration. There are various darknets you can use to access the "Dark Web", the otherwise impenetrable web you're not supposed to find.

You may have heard of file sharing software programs like Napster or LimeWire some years ago, and these are examples of one "darknet" type; a peer to peer network of users that share files. The "Deep Web" tends to encompass the darknet but the main difference is in the deliberate steps you must take to connect to the darknet.

The idea of the darknet actually precedes the "Deep Web", since the Darknet concept was devised in the 1970s, and referred to networks that were kept apart from ARPANET, which later became the worldwide connected Internet. The Deep Web resulted because of the need for resistance to an all searchable Internet. The Darknet concept simply evolved with the preference of privacy and more exclusive traffic.

The main difference between Deep and Dark is simply that a darknet doesn't have the classic "searchability" or even the *compatibility* to be loaded by unsuspecting users. If you tried to load darknet URLs provided by underground sources, you would not be able to load them simply by clicking the link in Internet Explorer, Firefox, Safari, Chrome and so on. The darknet is sometimes considered a portion of the Deep Web in technical terms, but in semantics, it is something far more guarded.

Later in this book, we're going to review the best ways to connect to the Dark Web as well as which ways are safest, which come with a risk and which programs are ideal for surfing anonymously.

Why the Surface Web is Extremely Limited

The question many people have when finding out that a "dark side of the Internet" exists, is why would you want to search information that is considered "secret"?

The easy answer is that the surface web is extremely limited in terms of providing information, and much in the same way as a TV network plans its schedule, there isn't much "exploring" to do on the surface web.

The surface web is highly guarded and filtered for public use. While some people from English-speaking countries may think that Darknet software programs are only useful to those living in communist countries, where the government controls Internet viewing, consider the facts about capitalist or socialist countries.

Google and Bing, as well as other English search engines, have all been known to manipulate their keyword search results for esoteric business reasons. Many believe that smaller websites are being suppressed by larger search engines in favor of well known brand name business. Furthermore, many of the news stories you see on the surface web are presenting one-sided information, as this stands to help various commercial or governmental purposes.

Part of the excitement of exploring the Dark Web comes from the idea that you could be reading stories or web pages that present a completely new perspective of life. Remember that in order to host a website on the surface web, most of the content published must be considered generally "mainstream". No hosting provider will allow a user to host content is considered too taboo, controversial or "alternative" in viewpoint.

Knowing this, it comes as no surprise that many users search darknets for underground political news, especially since many whistleblowing websites are now being censored from the surface web. Some hackers dream of being the next "big whistleblower", and imagine what information they might find by searching "secret" files that no one is supposed to read.

Some users prefer using a darknet to protect their own privacy and escape what they consider "mass surveillance" from invasive surface websites as well as the government.

Lastly, yes, the Darknet is sometimes used for illegal purposes, which might include hosting illegal stores, committing hacking crimes, sharing illegally acquired multimedia (new music and movies), or even distributing illegal pornography or scenes of real life murder. There is also much in the way of counterfeit software, identity theft and spam operations.

Last but not least, some enjoy surfing the dark web simply for the joy of finding something new and unexpected. Many sites on Darknet are harmless and somewhat trivial excursions into niche topics. Some web hosting users simply don't want to be searched or indexed and prefer anonymity. Others use the Darknet market to discover hard-to-find books that would probably not be published on Amazon, BN.com and other traditional stores.

BBS and Usenet Predecessors

Years ago in the 1980s and 1990s, Bulletin Board Systems were the predecessors of the online world. These were computer servers running custom software allowing anyone with a PC to connect to the system using a terminal. Once logged in, users were given access to a small community of users. Here, they could chat with each other, play games, read news items and share content without any third party company presiding over the process.

The BBS "Systems Operator" presided over the cyber-community using just a computer server, software and a phone line that directly connected users to the BBS. Sometimes the "sysops" who owned the BBS's would list phone numbers to other BBS's that you could call and connect to, for more exploring, file trading and news sharing.

Usenet groups were the next hike in technology and were repositories for discussion groups, connecting users from multiple locations and allowing file downloads and uploads and text discussions. Unlike the BBS or the modern day web servers, Usenet technology did not require a central server or dedicated administration. It existed via a forwarding news system that made use of multiple servers.

The deep and dark web essentially relive those old Usenet / BBS days, where users had access to an unfiltered, unregulated and largely unknown online world free from filtering and corporate-sponsored ads.

Is Surfing Darknet Legal or Illegal?

In surfing the Dark Web, you may discover something new that no one has ever seen before. You may find out something you never knew before or may catch a glimpse into an alternative lifestyle or political/religious point of view that you never knew existed.

You may stumble upon some illegal content, unfortunately, but there are ways to avoid that as we will discuss later. Lastly, you may and probably will discover many, MANY dead links. That's all just part of being an explorer into deep undiscovered territory.

The thrill of exploring the darkest parts of the web comes from venturing boldly into the unknown. Perhaps it's the closest we human beings can imagine to exploring space or the deepest part of the ocean. Half the thrill is searching for something undiscovered or stumbling upon a truly unique or mysterious page.

There is absolutely nothing illegal or unethical about exploring the darknet with a curious mind. You have every right to download software for exploring these "locked sites" and must use discretion if and when you do find something illegal. When in doubt, it's probably best to leave the page behind. And for more information on "what can go terribly wrong" be sure to check out our final chapter, which shares some of the more outrageous but still possible horror stories of deep web exploration.

For now, let's proceed onto the first chapter which discusses the only way to surf anonymously and safely if you're venturing into Darknet.

Chapter 2

The Only Ways to Surf Anonymously

For more information on WHY to surf anonymously, do read our later chapters which explain what often does go wrong when you innocently decide to stumble upon private web pages with unscrupulous owners. If a user does something illegal, local or federal authorities can sometimes catch them in the act, and it usually always involves users who forsook their anonymity by committing just one foolish mistake.

Even if your intentions in surfing are harmless, it's just not wise to expose your private information to various users around the world; and this information about yourself is stored in your home device(s), as well as your ISP connection, which contains your name, address, phone number and location, among other identifiers. It's also a bit empowering to surf the web anonymously free from targeted ads and without worry of having information stored on your computer.

The problem with using "anonymous browsers" on Firefox and Chrome "Incognito/Private" is that this only prevents your browsing history from being saved. However, just because your Internet activities aren't being recorded on YOUR PC doesn't mean it's anonymous. You're still leaving a trail behind.

Even users that are using the surface web might consider deleting cookies since these are tracking files that record information on you, and most browsers auto-accept cookies. Using the CCleaner program can clear cookies, but you need anti-tracking software to opt-out of all these ad networks that are scouting your online behavior. (Some popular programs for surface web anonymity include Privacy Badger, Ghostery, or Disconnect) Most people don't realize that these little "cookies" are basically following them around the Internet.

At some point, you're going to realize that just because you can wipe your device clean doesn't mean you're actually going to be anonymous in the eyes of others. Your actions can still be tracked and recorded by your Internet Service Provider.

There are two important steps for surfing the Darknet: connecting and anonymously surfing. Connecting to the Darknet requires either special software or configuring a proxy server.

You must use a private, anonymous browser to access the deep web. However, most users will use two means of anonymity, the second being a "virtual private network" that can mask your IP address which is the identifying information you leave behind. We will discuss the difference between these technologies in the next chapter.

In case you're wondering, it is possible to surf a darknet using your favorite browser like Firefox or Chrome. If you've ever tried to do this outright, you probably know that the browser will send a message stating that it cannot load the content. This is because ordinary browsers typically have high-level security and privacy settings, as well as a firewall set up to protect users from potentially unsafe sources. Additionally, the various web servers you encounter on the hidden internet may also have various security and privacy settings that you must adjust for, in order to access them.

There are ways to force an ordinary browser to become a dark web surfing tool. You would basically have to download TOR and then configure Chrome or Firefox to work with your new TOR-altered security settings; namely in proxy settings.

Most users would not attempt this, since it's easier and safer to simply install Tor and use a Tor-ready browser that guarantees anonymous browsing. Using an ordinary browser and constantly have to adjust, install, and turn on private browsing can also be a headache. Some plugins are now being offered for Firefox and Chrome and they reportedly block third-party cookies, do not store browsing or search history and block all trackers.

However, the most effective way to "go dark" when surfing Darknet is to download and use the TOR network plus browser. This is the focus of the next chapter.

Chapter 3

Pros and Cons of Using Tor

T.O.R. stands for The Onion Router and is not actually a browser but refers to a privacy network. TOR's main function is to let people surf the web without being tracked. The way this happens is that TOR bounces around your Internet traffic through an entire network of computer servers (or nodes). Therefore, the only IP addresses that show up are the ones of the exiting node—no way to pinpoint who exactly you are between each of the servers. That means the volunteer devices that are hosting the traffic will never actually record where the location is or where it's going. Only the exit IP.

That's the theory and though there are exceptions which we will discuss shortly, this is the primary "pro" for which to use TOR—a privacy network and actually a "browser bundle" of programs including a web browser created by the TOR people, aka Vidalia. This browser allows you to surf with peace of mind. TOR also has minimal plugins installed and other advanced security features.

Using TOR makes it difficult for people to track you but the primary con is that you must surf at a slower speed because of all the shared traffic. The traffic is encrypted inside of the TOR network, however, the TOR browser cannot encrypt your traffic between the TOR network and its final destination. This is why

VPN, or another method of encryption, is suggested for questionable final destination sites.

In like manner, TOR can also help users to host hidden services, if they want to create an app or website that has a hidden location, for other TOR users. All of these sites are not WWW friendly and thus end in an ".onion" address. Furthermore, these links are not keyword friendly and usually have random strings of characters so that they are difficult to find without a direct link or bookmark. The IP addresses have been hidden and they are not searchable by the surface web. What the TOR browser does is get the encrypted addresses ending in .onion (which signifies a TOR-compatible site) and then deciphers it for access.

TOR can be installed just like any other software and it works just like a web browser once the installation is complete. The TOR web browser is actually modeled after Firefox and thus it's not too hard to figure out. The official download site is at https://www.torproject.org/projects/torbrowser.html.en and because of the risk of malware, it's not recommended that you download from any other location besides the official site.

You can download the TOR bundle for Windows, Mac and Linux. Windows and Mac, however, have been called security risks by some users, prompting most in the community to recommend Linux, version Ubuntu or Unix Open Source. Linux is the official choice of government agencies when it comes to security.

Besides, users who are rightfully paranoid about being caught doing something questionable online have sought out additional security measures, such as installing T.A.I.L.S. (The Amnesiac Incognito Live System), an operating system designed exclusively for TOR and reportedly safer than a hard-drive setup of Windows or Mac. TAILS can be run on a "LiveCD USB stick".

How to Search the Deep Web

Browsing your darknet is usually a matter of following links, though some sources claim there are Onion-ready search engines that index content like (Onion.city, Onion.to, and NotEvil). However, you may actually get more information on "new" sites from borderline surface websites that aren't heavily moderated like Reddit, 4Chan and the like, by Reddit-searching for /r/deepweb, /r/onions, and /r/Tor pages.

Most users start their darknet surfing experience by visiting the surface web "Hidden Wiki" page (https://thehiddenwiki.org/), a page that lists direct URLs and a snippet of text indicating what the sites feature. This is a deep web news portal and you may find some fairly well known Deep Web search sites like DuckDuckGo, TORCH, and many others. Some sites are niche oriented, such as bitcoin services, while others claim to be torrent hosts and news sites.

Unfortunately for some reckless users who were more than ready to use the Darknet for illegal purposes, they quickly found out that sometimes TOR isn't enough to guarantee anonymity. Let's consider the value of VPN (Virtual Private Network) in the next chapter.

Chapter 4

Pros and Cons of VPN

The problem is that although TOR is an excellent tool for hiding your IP address, it is far from foolproof. There are end to end encryption issues that can compromise your anonymous web surfing. For that matter, if your IP address somehow escapes TOR privacy, (which can occasionally happen) your identifying information can be leaked, and that includes your location. That explains why law enforcement is able to invade the homes of "tracked" users and quickly find the evidence they need to arrest and convict those engaging in criminal activity. Some IP information can even reveal how often you visit particular sites; another piece of evidence required for prosecution.

This is why cautious users use Linux, T.A.I.L.S. LiveCD and TOR in addition to another staple of anonymity—the VPN or Virtual Private Network. A VPN works by way of establishing virtual point to point connections through dedicated connections; or alternately, virtual tunneling protocols or traffic encryption.

A VPN can mask a user's IP address and manually assign a fake IP address so that anyone examining it would see your location as another city, state, country or even across the world. In fact, every time you login to a VPN you receive a new IP address.

The "pros" of VPN include the ability to scramble a trail of logging evidence, and generally the higher the encryption bits (such 128 or 256 bit), the better. This at least prevents people from monitoring you and yes, even your ISP can monitor your usage and the sites you visit.

The Problem with Logging

Some VPN services, unfortunately, offer far more than they actually deliver. If the VPN company logs your usage, that's one thing—and many do. But some unscrupulous ones will actually make your loggings available to others without informing you.

Therefore one of the cons is that it's difficult to find a company that doesn't record logs, and even more difficult, or impossible, to find one that has no way of tracking your Internet usage. This gets tricky since in VPN marketing, everyone says they don't collect activity logging, even though they do.

For example, HideMyAss was one of the most trusted VPN providers in the world and claimed to never keep logs of its users. However, when the United Kingdom gave them a court order demanding them to provide logging records of a suspected hacker, they caved to the pressure.

The sad fact is that VPN companies are made of human beings just like you, and no one wants to go to jail when confronted with the option of cooperate or face the consequences. A customer's twenty dollar a month subscription is not much in face of millions of dollars of litigation.

HideMyAss's case proved that VPN networks DO log your activity, even though most will not sell it to just anyone. They are at the mercy of the courts, however, and so you do still have to be vigilant about leaving behind a trail of evidence.

The primary "pro" that can't be ignored regarding VPN is that they DO protect you from your own Internet Service Provider, if not the government. A VPN server can mask your ISP from monitoring your usage and even the fact that you're using TOR.

In theory, if the government is investigating you, one of the first visits they will make is your local ISP and they will certainly know if you use TOR; thereby giving a red flag to authorities that something may be going on. TOR isn't illegal by any means, but it does make people suspicious.

Now some people will actually use VPNs instead of TOR. It's definitely a good idea to use VPN if you're not using TOR, and that the VPN is using modern encryption methods as well. The opposite of an encrypted and well guarded Internet connection would be a public WI-FI network, which is very unsecure. In fact, VPN technology is so effective many Internet sites will block access to known VPNs.

Using TOR over a VPN does give you one layer of additional protection, since you can hide the fact that you use TOR from your ISP. All the VPN provider sees is that you do use TOR nodes and are sending encrypted data. They don't actually see what you are sending over this network.

Unfortunately for some users, VPN companies are still capable of decrypting data, checking and sharing logs with authorities and "betraying" you in lieu of a court order. Another con worth mentioning is that sometimes VPNs can drop connections without informing you, and if that's the case, the ISP can see your usage.

Just like TOR, VPNs are not foolproof even if they are an excellent way to double the strength of your anonymous connection. However, if you're determined to do something illegal or make a lot of enemies out on the Deep Web, then the next option might be a better plan: the Proxy Connection, which we'll discuss in the next chapter.

Chapter 5

Pros and Cons of Proxies

A proxy server refers to a computer server that is works as an intermediary, handling requests from other servers. One user connects to a proxy server, makes a request from a different server, and then proxy server evaluates the request. Open proxy servers are accessible by an Internet user. On the contrary, anonymous open proxy allows users to hide their IP addresses.

Compared to TOR, using a proxy server accomplishes many of the same functions, since the proxy server is configured for privacy and security, making the darknet accessible. Onion itself is a "proxy" and makes the darknet accessible. When used in the context of Proxy Vs. TOR Vs. VPN, this simply means that you don't have to use TOR if you distrust it. (And there may be a reason to)

You can use a different proxy server that performs the same function as TOR does. For example, Tor2Web is a fairly well known anonymous proxy server. However, their homepage Tor2Web.org states that they developed the proxy to be convenient and usable for publishers—not necessarily as effective as TOR when it comes to guaranteeing anonymity. Other proxies oft mentioned for darknet surfing include I2P, Freenet, Retroshare, Riffle, and GNUnet.

In theory, a proxy server will keep you anonymous in the same way as VPN and TOR, since it hides your IP address, the only difference being in the technology. The proxy is the gateway to the software you use it in. A proxy directs your traffic using another computer instead of your own.

The con here is that using anonymous proxy servers does not give you the extra of encrypted data. SOCKS and HTTP or proxies do not give any encryption, while HTTPS offers the same basic level of encryption as an SSL website.

Simply put, proxies were not made to hide your Internet traffic—only allow you to surf anonymously using a browser. Inferior proxies may even give away your original IP address, invalidating the whole process.

Proxies are single servers that refers incoming traffic away, removing certain information and replace it with different identifiers. The proxy server knows who you really are and if government officials can access the proxy, they can install monitoring software.

Proxy servers are typically used by people who have been spooked about using TOR, since there has been word of TOR having government spying "backdoors" built into the installation files.

One option might be to use a proxy server AND Tor, to help double the anonymity protection factor. This also obscures your location in case of monitoring.

However, it is important that you setup the proxy from inside TOR, rather than the other way around. Otherwise, TOR disables it. This adjustment requires configuring TOR Network Settings and then stating you want to use a proxy; from there, enter in a password and username and connect.

In summary:

TOR

Pro: Decentralized system, allowing the IP address hidden from each site by bouncing connection server to server. Encrypted data.

Con: Slow loading. The final connection point in the chain of servers could be revealed if the site doesn't use SSL, which is a possibility, since the TOR network cannot encrypt data between the TOR network and the final destination site. TOR is also notorious in name and using it may or may not tip the government off into monitoring you.

VPN

Pro: Changes your location via encrypted tunnel and masks your true IP information.

Con: Low quality VPN services can expose you to risk; efficient proper load balancing and server randomization is necessary to keep alternating your location. If your activity is logged, practically all VPN providers will turn evidence over to the authorities.

Proxy

Pro: More complicated setup, but will hide your IP address by directing traffic to other servers. Paid proxy servers are usually reliable.

Con: No encrypted data. Using Proxy and VPN can also cause more dramatic slowdown. It's strongly recommended to use VPN for encryption. May require proxy setup for multiple applications, such as email or browsing.

These are the most common ways people seek anonymity online. Now you may be wondering how secure can TOR, VPN or proxy be if people are following directions but still getting busted for illegal activities. The answers may surprise you as the next chapter explains.

Chapter 6

The Most Common Mistakes Made in Anonymous Surfing

Believe it or not, most people being busted on the Deep Web / darknet are simply making stupid mistakes, and rarely is it entirely the fault of the imperfect software. Consider for example some of the most common mistakes pedophiles and drug buyers make.

Ordinarily, law enforcement doesn't know where darknet websites are because of anonymizing software. They can barely start an investigation based on just one user's hearsay. However, many users stupidly leave comments on the surface web, such as YouTube, 4Chan, Reddit and so on.

Some will post pictures and forget that poor technique will leave metadata in the pictures, providing police more evidence to work with.

While it's hard to find encrypted data, it's fairly easy to take down drug stores with undercover agents posing as customers. Using snail mail addresses to ship drugs, guns or other illegal content can provide the physical evidence that police need to make an arrest. All it takes is an undercover agent to make the deal and a criminal investigation to dust for fingerprints, or to find drugs and paraphernalia.

Sometimes darknet users fall into the trap of using surface websites. For example, using a VPN but then entering your address on Google Map, sends traceable information to Google. Google, Facebook, and all the other local-centric sites log all information and they don't purge it.

Accidentally entering local information into a surface or "non-darknet Deep Website", while using a VPN, has compromised your security. Human error catches up with you quickly when performing illegal activities. If you're prone to human error, and plan on doing any espionage, then definitely use TOR as well as a VPN.

Less Common Mistakes

Bitcoins are sometimes the downfall of would-be anarchists, as bitcoin transaction records are public. Purchasing illegal goods can sometimes tie you to your surface web identity as well as other websites you visit.

Think about how you set up a bitcoin account—funding your account with a credit card, or PayPal account right? That's easily searchable for government agencies. Agencies can track down individual transactions based on specific bitcoin amounts traded.

One proposed solution is the invention of a new digital currency not associated with Bitcoin. Dashcoin is supposedly an anonymous currency, but it's not as widely accepted as Bitcoin.

Trusting People on Darknet

While there probably trustworthy people on the darknet, there are also plenty of bad guys…and plenty who will pretend to be your friend.

Onion sites, associated with TOR, do not make up the entire oceanic Deep Web. New Onion sites are somewhat easy to find and that means these sites are also easy for law enforcement to find, especially if you're using a well known site like The Hidden Wiki.

In order to entrap pedophiles, authorities are fighting back digitally as well as with undercover agents. Netherlands charity Terre des Hommes created a CGI bot that was designed to help lure pedophiles into conversation so they could be identified.

Using Public WI-FI

A surprisingly dumb move, and many people will actually ask questions online about setting up their TOR browser on a mobile phone. However, if you are in a neutral place like a library or café where you can have privacy, you don't actually have anonymity. The ISP of the establishment can track your usage and find hidden browser histories. All of these visits are logged. You also expose yourself to the threat of public photographs, proving you were at the location using the Internet. That's leaving physical evidence behind. Using darknet from a public WI-FI is an amateur mistake.

Using an Unsafe OS and Hard Drive

Windows is simply believed to be unsafe in comparison to Linux, because of a number of "back doors" that makes spying easy. A Linux OS, particularly one developed outside of your home country, would be the best way to deflect an investigation.

Even the users that work with Linux don't seem to understand how to use it properly. A hard drive operating systems is constantly storing files on the same drive as the OS. While there are OS's like TAILS, an even better idea is to simply use TAILS from a USB drive or DVD disc—no hard drive memory required. This is means less information your computer stores about your online habits.

Of course, just because you avoid the most obvious mistakes most users make doesn't mean you're in the clear yet. The truth is ever since whistleblowers have made headlines in world news, the NSA and other spying agencies, not to mention the FBI and state or county law enforcement are actively searching out people who may be performing illegal activity on the web.

The next chapter discusses the best way to avoid NSA spying.

Chapter 7

How to Avoid NSA Spying

First, let's review what will get you busted. Your IP address is sent somewhere whenever you decide to visit a website online, and your ISP has all the details on your IRL identity. No matter who you claim to be online or how many precautions you take, once the authorities have your ISP identifying information that's all they need to make an inquiry.

Government agencies have a power beyond ordinary sleuthing to spy on your online actions and understanding how they do it is essential to avoid becoming the next Julian Assange and living in a small embassy for the rest of your stressed life.

For example, it is believed that the NSA has the technical sophistication to decipher 1024 bit encrypted data. Private SSL or TLS protocols go up to about 512 bits. So even if you had 1024 bit encryption, one frequent problem is that Windows, Mac and Android users are sometimes forced to use 512 bits because of what is called a FREAK Attack (Factoring RSA Export Keys), an SSL TLS vulnerability.

The term Brute Force Decryption describes a deciphering threat that utilizes a computer with greater resources that is sure to overpower shorter encryption keys. Super computers owned by the government can easily overpower encryption if necessary—

so don't count on outsmarting the government in encryption software alone. NSA can also use something called "Grover's algorithm" and Shor's algorithm which can basically crack encryptions and search for single terms in private files.

If you're trying to hide from the NSA you're competing with "good guy" hackers and so their goal would be to break into your computer and recover evidence. Supposedly, some hackers believe that 2048 bit encryption as well as a stated "full security" from those super-algorithms would be something close to safe. Local law enforcement are obviously not as well equipped to spy on you to that level so they will spend more time using undercover agents and looking for common mistakes.

Another less common mistake is when you make the mistake of using an external drive without bothering to encrypt information. While it is a good idea to use a Flash drive in general, saving data on the drive or even a second external hard drive is not a completely foolproof plan.

External hard drives that connect to a computer are still accessible to the internal hard drive and processor, especially if the BIOS allow the master hard drive to scan all drives and keep logging records for maintenance. Even if you use a USB drive for saving files, they should always be encrypted.

Some hackers would also go so far as to recommend turning off scripts like Javascript, Flash and others, and using a minimal browser to avoid more threats.

Understand that if the NSA suspects you're a dangerous terrorist or whistleblower (Islamic, Australian or homegrown) they can and probably will try to decrypt your TOR data, although this would be a fairly uncommon scenario.

The bigger risk for you individually is that they will find you without needing your IP address at all. They may need it eventually to prove something in court, but they don't need it to start with. They can start an investigation with just your aggregated internet data, your so-called digital fingerprint. This collection of user information is stored on your browsing devices, and this identification can be aggregated and analyzed to identify a likely suspect. For example, plug-ins and browsers you use can leak data; everything from screen size to installed fonts and other small snippets of information and this can be organized into a case file that identifies you. This information can narrow you down out of millions of other users, who do not share your digital fingerprint.

Thus the alternative theory is that the more unique your user settings the clearer your digital fingerprint becomes to investigators. The goal then, some suggest, is to try to blend in with most other users and try not to configure your browser beyond the default.

When it comes to internet encryption, you are best served by using less well known, or even minimal browsers where you can shut off and other functions that can be vulnerable to hackers, who may be targeting you.

What About TOR Security Breaches?

Wouldn't the easy answer be to just use TOR and VPN together, upgrade your system and VPN provider software, and get to it? No, because as usual, the government is one step ahead. US Naval Intelligence practically invented TOR (or the technology that would evolve into TOR) for their own purposes, so you have to figure the government is smart—they know you're downloading TOR as a starting point and ARE watching you. How?

TOR operates by obfuscating IP address data, passing your information through other servers before you reach the final destination. At this time, the NSA still uses specialist code breakers to crack encrypted messages and this is a fairly complicated way to spy on people—meaning they don't have the resources to search every single person individually.

What's a much easier way to catch the most foolish amateur criminals? Make sure security breaches exist in computer devices and in programs, such as Mozilla, which aggregates digital fingerprints from users. The government practically admits to installing these "backdoor features" on devices, operating systems and websites (most notoriously Google, Facebook, Windows 10, etc).

The obvious question is, does the FBI, NSA or any government agency install back door spying software on TOR itself? It would certainly make sense, since the government designed the technology and since TOR is publicly and legally available to anyone that wants to download it.

That said, the belief is currently that TOR is not "loaded" with spyware. The government designed it so well that it seems to work just as it should—securely, protecting the user efficiently whether his actions are heroic or illegal. Edward Snowden recently stated that the NSA hasn't been able to compromise TOR as of yet, and that PROPER encryption is still proving to be the best way to avoid detection.

What might be happening with users who claim TOR is compromised, is that they are using TOR wisely but are leaving digital fingerprints in other ways. They blame it on TOR without realizing their other mistakes.

Local law enforcement, already limited in resources, probably (and correctly assumes) that most criminals are going to give themselves away soon enough by being overconfident or ignorant of the way anonymizing software works. Agents and police officials who are investigating someone look for human error first, and encryption cracking second.

TOR's Not the Problem—Your Hardware Might Be

If TOR is safe, which it probably is, then that still leaves plenty of technology open to tampering and that is what hackers believe is going on with the NSA at the moment. "Drive by downloads" refer to installing malware at high traffic sites for spying purposes; a staple of the cyber criminal, but now a method being used by government agencies to stop pedophiles, terrorists and others who may be using TOR to break the law.

Technological advances in combating cyber crime have been firmly in place for the last fifteen years or so and it's been well documented that a backdoor program can give the government access to the hardware device you use, regardless of TOR, which might include files, web history, location, device fingerprint, ISP and even your webcam.

Operation Torpedo

After years of governmental outcry over TOR's hard-to-crack function, there has been a great effort put forth to create a darknet crawler, one that could collect Tor onion addresses.

The agents working to arrest pedophiliac site owners got a breakthrough when they found a forum board with an open administrative account and no password. They logged in and found the server's IP address. Human error once again!

But there was one more smart move left by the FBI—they didn't immediately arrest the individual hosting the child porn sites.

They waited and spied on him and got all the search warrants and evidence they needed, and also modified the code on the servers to deliver their hacking tool to ANY other servers that accessed the sites under investigation. They not only got the primary host user but 25 additional visitors to the site. They subpoenaed all the ISPs involved and they got every last person's address, subscriber name and other personal information.

As you can see, there are many ways to circumvent TOR and many of them actually do just involve conducting surveillance on a suspected criminal, based on the FBI's own developed software that turns one's modern devices into spy tools.

Of course, comparatively, child porn and looking up "illegal information" for research purposes are hardly in the same league. It's easy to argue, legally speaking that one was looking at a news site or deep web link and stumbled upon private information. It's quite a different thing to be caught visiting a forum that advertises itself a Child Pornography Website. There isn't a lot of defense once the person has been caught, and lawyers of the accused person in this case, were unable to mount a legitimate defense based on the FBI's new method of surveillance.

Now where it will get complicated in the future is studying potential terrorists and whether they visited a terrorist website and if that implies guilt or premeditation of a crime.

There are certainly some activists in the IT industry that believe that the FBI's NIT (Network Investigative Technique) law-abiding malware is a dangerous precedent. In the future if the FBI is allowed to further scale up this NIT operation, they may be able to use remote access to search any and all electronic storage media and seize devices for investigation with little to no warning.

What Does This Mean About Your Darknet Experience?

Now all of this isn't suggesting that anonymity is impossible in this modern age. If the NIT was infiltrating every single device in existence and reporting back to the NSA / FBI in live time for review, obviously this book would be a lot shorter—we would just say "Don't bother surfing the darknet!"

But the truth of the matter is that just because the NSA has the capacity to find you in mere minutes, doesn't mean they have CAUSE to investigate you.

Knowing this information just emphasizes one of two logical scenarios: if you're going to use the darknet for legal purposes, fact finding and innocent browsing you won't have any problem. If one is going to use TOR for illegal purposes, he has to think like a criminal and that means using diligence in planning each and every move and securing every part of the process. Using TOR or a VPN is no longer an end-all to Internet security.

Investigators also have access to other modern digital identifiers, such as surveillance footage, facial recognition video hardware and software, and license plate recognition. Therefore, if you walk to a public place and peruse the darknet you're leaving behind a "video trail" with which you could be convicted, if doing anything illegal.

Some merchandise may also have a barcode or RFID chip installed, making it very easy to track the device itself, and thus find where you live and what location from which you access the Internet.

Once they have just a bit of evidence, all they have to do is make a realistic hypothesis; such as comparing your background history. You may or may not be on a watch list (nobody really knows what the FBI has on them) or even a terrorist screening database. If this is the case, you probably won't even know that you're being placed under surveillance and if you don't do anything illegal, then you probably won't ever hear of it. If you're already on a watch list and decide to do something blatantly stupid like collecting, storing or sharing illegal information, there won't be much problem in getting a warrant, arrest and conviction.

Stereotyping and profiling remain another unfortunate problem in many countries as law enforcement sometimes "profiles" a person, by relying on statistics, stereotypes or supposition trying to find patterns and motivations in a person's behavior.

Once they subpoena your IP information, they can also get far more details regarding your viewing habits, how long you looked at a page, how many pages were viewed and what you downloaded and stored.

What Silk Road 2.0 Taught Us

Let's pretend you're a criminal hoping to reach Silk Road notoriety (a fairly well known illegal drug and weapons store that was taken down); the case of Silk Road 2.0 should definitely intimidate you. The FBI, along with the cooperation of 17 other countries, over the course of six months ran Operation Onymous, which finally identified the source of Silk Road 2.0 (the re-launch of the banned site) and brought it down.

What's particularly interesting about this case is that no one actually knows how the government pulled this one off—and for good reason, since they may use their techniques again to bring down other criminal empires. No one shared any information, though some hackers and IT specialists speculate it could have been by finding TOR entry guards or exit nodes that they planted there. This would allow them to infiltrate the darknet structure and monitor snippets of traffic for evidence.

As we've seen, the darknet itself is just one avenue of exploration for government agencies. Email is a huge risk considering how it's easy to make a mistake in basic communication apart from TOR. Let's review email anonymity in the next chapter.

Chapter 8

Anonymous Email

Popular email clients may be secure but they're not darknet secure. The most popular email websites are well known to log information about all of their visitors and account holders, from Facebook to Gmail to Yahoo, MSN and others. The fact that they let you access email remotely also means that they may be keeping records of your online behavior and saving all correspondence—identifying your fingerprint at the word of dozens of remote sites you used to access your webmail.

Formerly, darknet mail had a mainstay: TOR mail but when its former host Freedom Hosting left the scene so did TOR Mail. Some speculate that all those mail messages may have been confiscated and are being read for investigation by the government—or perhaps they've fallen into criminal hands. They're simply gone.

Of course, people who are smart about remaining anonymous don't use clear text email but will instead use encryption software to protect all of their text. The majority of criminals still don't use encrypted email which just shows you the recklessness of some of these TOR users intent on breaking the law.

Think of the security risks it would pose if one person has a list of secret contacts, and then one of those contacts replies to everyone using clear text email without encryption. It would be a major security breach and beyond the control of most of that contact list.

Some of the popular email and messaging encrypted software include BitMessage, TorChat, 12P-Bote and MixMail.

The idea behind this darknet mail is that you can receive messages without revealing your location or digital fingerprint. Many darknet mail clients and users will state to you that there definitely is a different among providers; some offerings are unsecure, unreliable and not as private as they should be. Paid email services are available via Bitcoin or another form of digital currency. The company might also claim to never keep any logs, and thus can claim ignorance as to whatever is being encrypted and sent.

One company known as SIGAINT stated in an interview that they hold all correspondence in a secret physical location that is part of the TOR network and operate two expendable proxies that tunnel mail from the clearnet (public internet) back to the secret data warehouse using TOR. They say that private data warehousing prevents tampered-with hardware; no virtual servers are used.

Another factor that keeps them and other darknet email options viable: the operators of the service are also anonymous, meaning they can't be found and forced to give logs even if they had them, which they don't. Even when law enforcement questions them informally, they can accurately state they have no way of retrieving encrypted information. The fact that police can't determine who legally owns the service prevents most investigations from pressing forward.

Even with all this information, it still should be noted that if child exploitation is reported to the company, they will delete the offending email account. Besides the pedophile community itself, there simply isn't much tolerance for any child abuse from even the most mysterious and rebellious darknet users.

In the next chapter we're going to discuss what to do if you suspect surveillance and need to delete all evidence from your device.

Chapter 9

Getting Rid of Evidence and History (and Why You Might Want To)

By now you've figured out that surface web software or surface browsers like Firefox and Chrome probably won't do much to remove your browsing history, even if they do promise to scrub your device.

Some programs like CCleaner may be able to delete traces of files left by various browsers as well as other file formats. File Shredder, Eraser, and Zilla Data Nuker are also popular choices. The manual deletion software may be able to delete files and prevent recovery software from restoring them.

Some of these software programs can also delete related cookies, recycle bin files, memory dumps, fragments of files, log files and application data, and other tidbits. The registry cleaner included also corrects problems with Windows registry, and the missing file logs that can result from deleting an important file. This computer software is recommended if you're going to sell your computer to someone else or if you have any other reason to delete files or browsing history.

However, a better way to ensure the complete removal of all stored files would be "wipe" the hard drive and get rid of all trails of said files. Remove all former data and operating system information by replacing each bit of data with blank data. This is the official plan of government agencies who have to dispose of sensitive information.

Remember to also delete wireless network keys or passphrases, network share passwords and another passwords for VPN or dial-up. Disabling the System Restore feature of Windows is also required.

The faster way would simply be to delete the entire hard drive, meaning it would need a new installation of an operating system to return to normal function. Programs like Disk Wipe can erase drive partitions but only if the drive is placed inside another computer. To destroy the main system disk of your PC you need a bootable disc or USB drive that can create a boot and then complete erase and format the drive's partitions. Active@ Kill Disk is program that can assist with wiping a hard drive.

Tablets and Smartphones

While each phone has an accessible "Clear History" feature in the settings, you may be rightfully paranoid about some evidence left behind. If you want to completely scrub your cell phone or tablet, running on an Android OS, you have to do something MORE than clearing history and even more than a factory reset. Otherwise, your phone will still yield old photos, emails, messages and searches. A factory reset only deletes addresses of data; but it doesn't overwrite the data.

The first step to destroying the memory of an Android unit is to encrypt the data. This option is built into the system and requires a PIN. Anyone that tries to recover info now will be stuck because they can't decrypt it without a special key. While encrypting data, keep it plugged in because it will take considerable time. If you need help finding the option, it should be somewhere in the settings/lock and security menu. You may also want to encrypt the SD card.

This function was built with the intent of preventing thieves from stealing the phone and then using any valuable information on it. Bear in mind some phones or tablets may require a user name and password for the last Google account registered on the system. Not having any information may lock the phone entirely. Therefore, turn off lock on the security feature before starting.

The next step is to remove your Google account, which in accessible from the Accounts and Sync menu. Now you will actually perform the factory reset by accessing it from Settings / backup and reset.

After this, the phone is wiped and any leftover data that could still be on there will be encrypted and protected. If you still have doubts about it try overwriting the encrypted data with new information (such as large videos) and then doing another factory reset repeating the same steps.

When it comes to wiping an Apple product, understand that these iOS devices are hardware encrypted, which means it has better privacy protection than normal.

Sign out of Facetime, iMessage and iTunes. General reset resets all passcodes but to be safe choose "disable restrictions" and then "erase all contents and settings". You will be prompted for your passcode and password, in order to turn off the locking feature. This process allows you to set up a new device. Unregistering your device can be done through the site at supportprofile.apple.com.

Be sure to delete additional information from your iCloud account and make sure you sign out before erasing the data. You can also delete your information remotely even if you don't have the device anymore, by using iCloud and the "Find my iPhone" feature, which lets you erase it from the cloud. From the cloud you can also remove debit or credit card information. Deleting iCloud account information (like contacts, calendars and photo streams) is so effective Apple actually advises against it, suggesting that there's no way to restore them.

ISP Logging

There is one last agency to worry about and that's your local ISP provider and this is very often the weakest link that gets users in trouble. ISP companies sell you out quickly so the best case scenario is to use anonymizing software and then count on the predictable practice of ISP providers purging their records.

There are no data retention laws in the U.S. specifying a certain time that companies must keep old records, however this could change in the near future as the U.S. may follow the example of Europe and introduce legislation requiring old records to date back to at least a year.

Most ISPs are not extremely supportive of government agencies in that they don't make it a point to keep logs for an excessively long time. Some might state they delete the logs every two weeks; others may never share that information. Larger providers are a tad more cooperative, like Time Warner Cable who stores IP address logs up to six months, or Comcast for three months. Charter stores for up to a year while Cox stores for six months. Smartphone Internet providers may keep records for longer periods of time, up to one year, such as in the case of Qwest/Century, and AT&T. Verizon went above the standard and states they hold records up to 18 months.

Unfortunately for law breakers, these records would serve as evidence and a person wouldn't be in the clear for the entire duration of that time period in which log records are kept.

We've mentioned a few things in passing that you might find on the darknet. But just what kind of horrors are we talking about? Perhaps not as horrific as you've heard... in the next chapter we'll discuss some of what you might find on the darknet as well as a few of the more absurd myths.

Chapter 10

What You Might Find on the Dark Market

Exploring the dark web is just as legal as exploring the surface web and all anonymizing browsers are free to download, no secret password or club required.

What gets tricky is determining what actions are illegal, and usually ignorance is not a good defense in this case, since users have to take very specific actions to (a) download the anonymizing browser and (b) do the illegal activity.

The most common illegal activities on the deep web are fairly self-explanatory and predictable:

1. Downloading new movies, software or music

"Torrenting" multimedia that is still being sold legally is highly illegal. Unless the creator gives the public permission to download (usually a small developer or new musician trying to go viral) the content should not be downloaded. Over 98% of all Torrent downloads are for illegally acquired movies, software, TV shows and music.

Many people do this even on the regular deep or surface web, and are simply ignorant of their law breaking or correctly figure they probably won't get caught.

Users who break the law in this regard avoid detection by checking their downloading speed and size and making sure it's not too high, as this may get noticed by authorities.

2. Enjoying and storing extreme pornography

You can probably find questionable pornography on the surface web, or perhaps the deep web—such as incest, bestiality or (fake) rape videos. Some countries prohibit violent pornography.

In the United States, for example, federal laws do not prohibit animal pornography but state laws may be applied to producers and performers of such videos. However, it is usually not considered a crime to watch "questionable" pornography, especially considering the difficulty of obtaining a police warrant to search exclusively for bestiality porn.

On the other hand...enjoying child pornography is highly illegal and a major risk, because law enforcement, federal and state level, is constantly searching for pedophiles and finding new ways to catch them in a cyber-crime.

Child pornography, whether violent in nature, sexually explicit or even supposedly "innocent" is all considered highly illegal and can lead to prison sentences if authorities find evidence on your computer of consistent downloading, storing and viewing of these shocking images.

Child porn is specially targeted by police because it is a form of human trafficking and the buying into the market for these images and videos only helps to further kidnapping, sexual exploitation of minors and other means of coercion.

Many people surfing Darknet stumble upon child pornography sites by accident and then wonder if they've committed a crime in doing so. Accidentally viewing an offensive picture and then quickly leaving the site is certainly not on the same level as accidentally seeing an image and then seeking out more images—perhaps even storing said images on a computer. Police will search for this trail of evidence when invading an accused person's home with a warrant. It's hard to press charges for accidentally viewing one image by accident (and promptly deleting all history)—but it's easy to make a case against a pedophile who collects many images and videos.

Some forms of victimless extreme erotica (such as text-only stories involving children or cartoon depictions of underage sex) may not be considered universally illegal and may actually be accessible on the regular deep web, or even some pornographic surface websites. However, there have been cases of individuals being sued or arrested for accidentally taking pictures of animated child sex into the public eye and the image later being discovered. This is why many surface websites will not publish questionable content, because the practice may violate some state laws.

The easiest way to avoid legal problems is to NOT click on any site that offers links to CP or Child Porn (since clicking on the link would imply intent to view in court) and to immediately leave any site that shows child porn.

3. Real Murder

So-called snuff videos, whether they are real or fake, sound highly disturbing and some users have claimed to have found these videos from obscure deep web links. The legality of viewing these videos is questionable, if not as concrete as that of child pornography. For example, some surface web videos show the real life depictions of savage murders and it would not be considered illegal to view them. However, if police raided your home and found virtual libraries full of darknet-acquired snuff videos, it may not bode well for you—at the very least it might paint you as a terrorist suspect. If it could be proven that you chatted with others or interacted in some way with the murderer in real time, or assisted in someone's death, a case could be certainly be made, if authorities chose to investigate.

Most people who view these videos suffer from some minor form of PTSD (Posttraumatic stress disorder) afterwards, so regardless, it's certainly not advised.

4. Sharing or viewing confidential files

This another avenue that's hard to classify, but if it became known that you willfully viewed, stored or shared confidential files with the public, or among friends, you could theoretically be sued or arrested for hacking crimes, or worse yet, meet the same fate as Julian Assange or Edward Snowden.

Some well known companies have had confidential records exposed publicly by anonymous hackers, such as the Ashley Madison website. Viewing these records would not necessarily be illegal, since they do not involve malicious intent. On the other hand, supporting stalking websites or identity theft websites, would certainly demonstrate willful criminal intent.

5. Committing certain Bitcoin-related actions

Bitcoins themselves are not illegal but many things that people buy using Bitcoins can be illegal, from drugs to hookers to weapons. Manipulating currency or fraudulent schemes involving Bitcoins is also highly illegal. Making income from Bitcoin but not reporting it to the IRS is also illegal. Anything to do with creating a new credit report or any financial fraud would likewise be a huge risk.

6. Hiring hit men and other human trafficking

While it's doubtful some of the assassins online are real (would they really advertise it and risk getting caught?) it is still illegal to hire someone for murder, or for any form of human trafficking. It's not necessarily illegal to view these websites but highly illegal to order from them.

Most of them are probably scam artists who simply create a sensational web page and then accept your bitcoin money. After all, if the murderer decides he doesn't want to the job after getting your money who are you honestly going to complain to? The urban legend goes that the hitmen for hire will key anyone who is of legal age and who isn't "top 10" famous.

There have also been rumored to be science experiment websites, which broadcast footage of animal or human experimentation. Some of these are said to be interactive, with paying users able to decide the level and degree of torture. While these sites are not commonly found, do keep in mind they would be rather easy to fake, as there are many movies selling footage of "death" that have been debunked as staged, such as the *Faces of Death* series.

7. Buying drugs or illegal weaponry

Interacting with drug stores on the Darknet is illegal and these transactions oftentimes lead to customers getting caught by police. Automatic weapons are also offered at some of these stores, as well as confidential financial records. The follow up of postage mail coinciding with the online order is sometimes what exposes these careless users.

There are of course many grey areas in deep and dark web surfing; many users describe strange forums and websites they have uncovered, from slave trading to child trading or supposed "cannibal forums", which would seem illegal in theory, (or at least the actions described would be illegal). However, viewing these strange pages would probably not constitute a crime. Obviously, if you start to uncover disturbing details or images, use your own discretion in determining if such content might be illegal or sadistic in nature and then leave for the sake of your somewhat innocent mind.

8. Strange Forums

Forums on the surface web have fairly tight regulations as to what can be said or shared about a person's private life. Not so with forums on the darknet which may include all sorts of strange support groups from illegal adoption (offering a child for trade or sale) or even mothers who have lost their fetuses and wish to share photographs. Cannibal cafes are also around, though it's likely that these violent forums—as well as many others like them, exist primarily as a means of fantasy exchange. Some users simply like to imagine themselves as murderers for their own aggrandizing purposes, and no surface web forum in their right mind would allow them to publish their unfiltered thoughts.

Viewing these forums is probably not illegal per se, so as long as no one posts illegal photos. However, they may be very disturbing if you're only used to watching fairly normal people interact on Facebook.

9. Prostitutes

It's not as far-fetched that you might meet a professional "illegal contractor" on the deep web, since criminal activity is far more common and profitable than murder, which seems rather extreme. For example prostitutes outside Nevada (the non-escort variety) may have pages on the deep web, where they can explicitly talk about their services. This would be in violation of the guidelines of any surface website, and so the deep web would be a haven for that. With Craigslist banning escort ads a while back, it's reasonable to believe prostitutes might be hiding on the deep web with more explicit advertised services.

10. Hackers and Cyber Criminals

Likewise, hackers and black hat SEO quasi-professionals may advertise their services here, as there are many hackers who can recover money, take down popular websites, steal financial information, and engage in all sorts of shenanigans. Some contractors might offer to install malware for a price, or develop spyware that is against the law.

11. Surface Websites Posing as Deep Web Sites

Here's something else you might find, ridiculous websites claiming to offer knowledge on summoning demons. All of this stuff, as well as Illuminati documents, are (hopefully?) fake and the embarrassing truth is you could probably find them on the surface web as most publishers and hosts don't really care what wacky religious ideas you preach, so as long as no pedophilia is involved.

While it may not be entirely legal to advertise your house and look for roommates, at a deep web site like Grabhouse that's basically what you get—though you could probably find broker-free living accommodations on Craigslist as well.

12. Strange Video Games

Perhaps the most documented "Dark Web Video Game" is that of Sad Satan. This was a rather esoteric RPG game with somewhat dated graphics, but one that raised controversy when people began speculating it was some sort of pedophilia inspired game. Some users claim the video game is on the deep web and it's been altered to include child porn images or footage of real death. However, most of the footage you can find of it on YouTube only contains strange photos and a somewhat incoherent narrative.

While not every game sounds as menacing as Sad Satan, if you look long enough you're bound to run into something bizarre and unsettling.

13. Legal Professionals Without Ethics

Lastly, there are unconfirmed reports of doctors, lawyers, customs officials and otherwise legal professionals who can be bought for illegal purposes. For examples, discreet doctors that can perform illegal late term abortions in certain states. Or, crooked police officers that can arrange a hit. Much of this is unproven and hearsay, though it's certainly not out of the question that favors can be bought.

If you really want to take a risk, you can always hire a non-certified professional, such as a quack doctor, to perform a high-risk operation. This isn't too far-fetched of a story, considering that there are probably plenty of doctors, lawyers and professors who are not authorized to practice their specialty by law, but still want to make extra money.

Here's one you might not have thought about: exotic pets. It's illegal to own certain wild animals in most jurisdictions. So why not order that lion off the deep web?

What You Probably Won't Find on the Deep Web

Sorry to break your heart, but so-called top secret files of governments admitting shocking conspiracies or real Illuminati footage would be next to impossible to discover, or would be hoaxes. The simple reason being that if such top secret meetings were taking place, they would likely not be recorded by anyone and shared on an obscure deep web URL.

Wikileaks may well be the most cutting edge website publishing controversial news leaks and it has gained notoriety for its accuracy. More obscure sites could easily doctor photos or even make up *National Enquirer* like headlines that have no basis in fact. You can certainly uncover some interesting gossip about people, places and things on the Dark Web...but then again, some of this content is just as easily available on the surface web on a site like Reddit, because hearsay is not that controversial.

User posts on the Deep Web or surface web may occasionally refer to stories being suppressed by the traditional media because of the threat of scandal or even libel. No traditional news website wants to risk a lawsuit by going against the grain. In like manner, banned videos, as well as porn that is classified as "revenge porn" and thus illegal for most surface websites, could be more easily accessed on the darknet.

Supposedly a Level 5 exists on the darknet somewhere, which could reveal super top secret information like "Tesla's experiments", the location of Atlantis, CIA secrets, or the legendary Mariana's Web, named after the deepest ocean trench. Mariana's Web has been called the Internet equivalent of the Vatican archives, a mysterious holy grail of knowledge.

Another bizarre theory is that Mariana's Web is a superintelligent AI (female of course) that has become self-aware and now overlooks the Internet as some type of God-like being. Here's the kicker: to access this VIP information would require something called Polymeric Falcighol Derivation, which necessitates using a quantum computer, which doesn't yet exist.

What you might actually find on the Deep Web are a bunch of trolls who claim to know something, or have seen something, but not actually provide any proof—sort of like the ordinary deep web or the surface web.

Here's a new thought courtesy of WIRED, which sought to debunk prevalent Deep Web myths. A review from the Internet Watch Foundation discovered that of all 30,000+ URLs that contained child pornography, only 0.2 percent were hosted on the dark web.

In terms of banned books, the first amendment protects against the banishment of books that are controversial in nature—even though publishing companies like Amazon exercise their right to censor far more often. Even so, censorship 2.0 still exists in a form, and it is usually by way of suppressing books by threats of litigation or dismissing legitimate suppositions as conspiracy theories. In this manner, there are "banned books" on the deep web—perhaps books that traditional publishing houses didn't wish to publish for legal reasons. Perhaps even books that no independent website wants to host for fear of being sued, like "How to Cook Humans" or "How to Make a Bomb" or something similarly macabre.

So yes, books are banned but not for obscenity—just for the far more real threat of libel.

How Do You Report Illegal Activity on Darknet?

Let's say after surfing the darknet for days on end you finally hit the motherlode: a real snuff murder site! You're appalled and disgusted. What do you do? Your first instinct is to call the police right?

Not a great idea, since by the time you actually call the police and get them to come over and look at the computer that site might be long gone. Furthermore, just because a site is accessible for the time being doesn't mean it's traceable. Local law enforcement is only interested in an emergency; meaning you are in immediate danger, not someone halfway across the world.

What about the option to report the site to the FBI? This is much easier to do when it's on the surface web. On the darknet, it's most complicated. Most illegal sites are well hidden with proxy servers and may only be accessible with a referral address and password, not a search or regular link listing.

Believe that the FBI is aware of these types of sites existing and they do occasionally find publishers and distributors and seize their servers when they get enough evidence to charge someone. The problem is these sites are very difficult to locate and it's not just a matter of gathering a URL. All you can control is your own actions, so make a conscious effort not to view anything illegal, or inadvertently supporting human trafficking by encouraging their activities.

Chapter 11

What Else Can Go Terribly Wrong?

Aside from the "temptation" to engage in illegal activity, you could run the risk of accidentally falling into a trap. While it's easy to avoid keywords that advertise illegal pages (beware of "CP", "PD", "jailbait" or "Hard Candy) you may occasionally get requests to download a mysterious file, especially from untrustworthy websites. Refuse the download and be sure to avoid that site in the future.

The same is true of webpages that advertise one thing but end up redirecting you to a porn site you didn't ask for. Click back and blacklist that site. There are two ways to avoid accidentally seeing child porn, if that's your worry—and it is a legitimate worry, because no one wants to be falsely accused of that!

Either limit yourself to deep web search engines that avoid listing any sites known to distribute CP (examples might include Complete Planet, TechXtra and InfoMine) or install an Image Block add-on (available through TOR-enhanced Firefox) to stop auto-loading all pictures. Or you can look inside the TOR browser and adjust the performance settings, where you can block scripts from loading. This may prevent you from accidentally seeing a horrible image you didn't ask to see.

Avoiding Viruses and Malware

Viruses are a huge risk on the darknet since you're talking about ungoverned Internet space here. A strong anti-virus program is recommended for deep web exploration, because as many users note, one of the most common risks is not really the FBI knocking at your door, but of you accidentally installing malware at a variety of untrustworthy websites.

Of course, many experienced users will tell you that even on the surface web, anti-virus programs are far from 100% effective. In fact, the best way to not download a malicious piece of software is to not use sites that are untrustworthy. One obvious protection is to not use any Windows computer, but to use a Linux OS instead, which is less prone to malware. The TOR browser has an option to turn off scripts like Java and Flash and so protect you from that kind of hijacking malware. Using Linux it's unlikely you will run into any malware since statistically we're talking about a 1% chance. Linux is well protected and usually requires a root password to install a new program.

For those foolish enough to use a Windows system, they are at a greater risk of contracting a "computer STD". Three of the most popular malware programs known to be on the darknet or deep web include Vawtrack, which gives hackers access to your financial records; Skynet, which steals your bitcoins, another Skynet operation called DDoS (Distributed Denial of Service) which attacks other sites using your infected computer, and

Nionspy, which can steal documents, spy on your keystrokes, or even record audio and video from your computer—usually a laptop.

These malware programs are probably to blame in various deep web horror stories where you hear about an innocent surfer getting his laptop hijacked and his web cam operating with a mind of its own. In theory, yes it's possible but only if the user is ignorant of security risks. Mainly, using Windows or not disabling scripts before venturing out.

If you're planning to download any files from a darknet, simply disconnect your Internet before running these files, since viruses would require an Internet connection to completely install.

In theory, even a Linux system is at a slight risk of a malware job, and if this is the case a hijacking of your computer would require something called a RAT, a Remote Administration Tool. After breaking into your system using a gateway program (which requires an Internet connection and preferably through a script) a hacker could use the RAT to "take over" your controls—and video tape you or issue threats, etc.

It's just much harder to find a gateway if you have Linux and all scripts disabled. The hacker really has to be smart at that point, and you're just as likely to run into the government as you are a super smart hacker that just hates you for no reason.

One theory is that using a well known program like Skype may put you at a slightly higher risk because Skype is an app and not as secure as a simple Linux and TOR setup.

If you don't have SSL or TLS encryption installed then there are security risks at the exit node (server) in the TOR network. For example, if you login to a website or an app that *bypasses TOR*, (usually a plugin / script) then you're at risk once again. The encryption of your data on the final destination website depends upon the settings of that website! This is why programs like HTTPS Everywhere can help.

Being unaware of this fact explains some Deep Web horror stories where users using TOR were shocked to discover that system administrators of a strange new website could trace their IP addresses and read all of their personal information. It's not safe if the strange website itself is figuring out how to bypass TOR's secure settings within the network.

Also, many users when using TOR forget the extra step to delete / turn off cookies and all local data after visiting a site, since this can reveal some of your digital fingerprint. One add on called Self-Destructing Cookies can auto delete cookies and prevent this security breach.

Recently, it's been observed that using the TOR Browser Bundle (which includes a TOR-compatible Firefox) may be compromised by government agencies, and particularly for Windows users.

As we've learned there are plenty of things that can go wrong when using TOR, but they are often exaggerated when you read Deep Web horror stories. The bottom line is that you're unlikely to stumble upon something ghastly if you take basic precautions and don't go looking for trouble.

After all, going to visit some criminal's website, being outraged, and then telling him you're going to report him to the police...not the smartest thing to do, all things considered.

Conclusion

We've come to the end of this book, though we have certainly not discovered the "End of the Internet", which as we've learned does seem to go on indefinitely. As we've learned, there is nothing inherently wrong with surfing the darknet / Deep Web, and even if supposedly the government knows you're downloading TOR, there's very little risk of you being dragged off to jail if you stay away from the most blatant pornographic websites.

Many on the surface web will tell you that the Deep Web Horror stories you read online are mostly urban legends, and it's actually quite unlikely you're going to stumble upon a red room featuring Live Human Experiments.

On the other hand, if you're easily disturbed at the secret thoughts of your fellow man, finding a cannibal forum or dead fetus forum, may be just enough to scare you off the deep web entirely. What the darknet gives you, and authors / readers like you, is freedom—a chance to look at the unfiltered lives of people and their darkest motivations.

While it's true that there are 500 more websites on the darknet than on the surface web, most of these sites are not criminal in nature, and some of them are actually quite tedious—or consist of mostly broken links.

So if curiosity is killing you, go ahead and download TOR and have a look around. You might actually find that the darknet isn't nearly as much of a red light district as you heard. But who knows…maybe you'll stumble upon something interesting one day and it will give you an idea on how to develop your own "Deep Web Horror Story".

Just remember to make it entertaining because everyone loves a tall tale!

www.ingramcontent.com/pod-product-compliance
Lightning Source LLC
La Vergne TN
LVHW052312060326
832902LV00021B/3839